BASEBALL

THOMAS S. OWENS
DIANA STAR HELMER

TWENTY-FIRST CENTURY BOOKS

BRO

To Judith Prowse Buskirk and B.B. Buskirk, who are always cheering as we swing for the fences

Cover photograph courtesy of © Allsport USA (Nathan Bilow)

Photographs courtesy of © Allsport USA: pp. 7 (David Seelig), 16 (Andy Lyons), 26 (Otto Greule), 28 (top, Rick Stewart; bottom, Tom Warshaw), 37 (Jeff Carlick), 42 (Brian Bahr); SportsChrome USA: pp. 8, 23 (© Rob Tringali, Jr.), 24 (© Rob Tringali, Jr.); National Baseball Hall of Fame Library & Archive, Cooperstown, N. Y.: pp. 11, 49 (Milo Stewart, Jr.); St. Paul Saints: p. 13; Reuters/Archive Photos: pp. 18 (Ron Kuntz), 48 (Tim Parker), 51 (Sue Ogrocki), 53 (Jeff Vinnick); UPI/Corbis-Bettmann: pp. 21, 32, 39; AP/Wide World Photos: pp. 34, 43

Designed by Molly Heron

Owens, Tom, 1960-
    Baseball / by Thomas S. Owens and Diana Star Helmer.
    p. cm. — (Game Plan)
    Includes index.
    Summary: Describes how professional baseball teams prepare
for games, analyze the games afterwards for improvement, develop strategies,
and build themselves through player selection.
    ISBN 0-7613-1373-7 (lib. bdg.)
    1. Baseball—United States—Juvenile literature. [1. Baseball.]
I. Helmer, Diana Star, 1962- . II. Title. III. Series: Owens, Tom, 1960- Game Plan.
GV863.A10934   1999
796.357'0973—dc21   98-43523   CIP
                                                       AC

Published by Twenty-First Century Books
A Division of The Millbrook Press, Inc.
2 Old New Milford Road
Brookfield, Connecticut 06804

CONTENTS

JUST ANOTHER GAME?

1

On May 17, 1998, the baseball season was barely six weeks old. No team was a sure contender for the championship. The midseason All-Star teams hadn't been chosen. The only sure thing was that every baseball game counted in the march to the World Series. Players like David "Boomer" Wells knew it.

As Wells warmed up for the game, Yankees manager Joe Torre asked pitching coach Mel Stottlemyre how their starter looked. Stottlemyre had a simple answer.

"Wow!" was all that Stottlemyre said.

Wow? For Wells?

According to the media, Wells was a wild-and-crazy personality, someone who didn't worry much about physical fitness. His weight seemed to seesaw. Newspapers hinted that Yankees coaches and even team owner George Steinbrenner worried about Wells. Sure, the lefty's record was 4-1 so far this season, but every game he started was a surprise. Once he had pitched wearing a 1934 cap previously owned by Babe Ruth, estimated to be worth $35,000.

A wild personality, perhaps. But a wild pitcher? Not Wells. He had worked ten years in professional baseball as a reliever before blossoming as a starter for the 1993 Detroit Tigers. Pitching close to 200 innings per season gave Wells a reputation as a "workhorse," plus a chance to show off his pinpoint control. But even Wells's control made him unpredictable. Since batters could count on a good pitch, Wells often gave up more hits and homers than wilder throwers might.

BEANIE BABIES ATTEND

The year before, Wells's 16–10 record had seemed terrific, until he lost five straight during New York's 1997 pennant chase. Some reporters predicted that Wells's best was behind him. Nevertheless, more than 49,000 people filled Yankee Stadium as Wells started against the Minnesota Twins that day. It was a great day for a ball game—cloudy, 59 degrees, a light wind. But the crowd wasn't thinking about Wells, the weather, or even the Yankees, who were first place in their division. Most folks were there for the team giveaway, a Beanie Baby toy bear named Valentino.

By the third inning, Wells had everyone thinking about baseball.

Minnesota's Jon Shave and Javier Valentin froze, stopped by called third strikes. Pat Meares struck out swinging, fooled by a change-of-pace pitch. Wells would register 11 strikeouts that day, and with his teammates gobbling up every Minnesota hit, Wells was on his way to a perfect game: 27 batters up, 27 batters down, and not one reaching base.

Pitchers often get most of the credit for perfect games. But Yankee catcher Jorge Posada masterminded the game plan against Minnesota that day. Posada "called" the game, using hand signals to ask Wells to throw certain pitches to certain Twins. Later, Posada raved to journalists about how Wells mixed four different pitches for strikeouts: a fastball, a curveball, a "cut" fastball (known by many as a slider), and a change-up. The catcher said he asked Wells to work the inside and outside corners of the plate, keeping pitches low and harder to reach. The lefty displayed perfect control, yielding not a single walk. Posada marveled at how many quick two-strike counts Wells achieved to stay ahead of most Minnesota hitters. But in the

> . . . .
> **The only two Yankees ever to pitch perfect games at home, Don Larsen and David Wells, both attended California's Point Loma High School.**

David Wells of the N.Y. Yankees is on his way to pitching a perfect game against the Minnesota Twins on May 17, 1998.

seventh inning, fans feared for the perfect game when Paul Molitor, the Twins' best hitter, took Wells to a count of three balls, one strike. The pitcher battled back and finally struck him out.

SAVING THE DAY

With one out in the eighth inning, Minnesota had its best chance to spoil Wells's masterpiece-in-the-making. Ron Coomer connected on an outside fastball, belting a line drive to second baseman Chuck

Knoblauch. The pitcher later said he was sure the Twin had ripped a single up the middle.

Infielder Knoblauch had other ideas. Staying in front of the ball, he downed the hit and threw out Coomer with time to spare. "If I catch it, I catch it. If not, I knock it down," Knoblauch said of his defensive game plan. Knock it down? "When it's hit hard, you have time" to get the throw back to the infield, he said. Even the fastest runner doesn't move as quickly as a hard-hit ball.

The ninth inning arrived, and the possibility of a perfect game was no secret. The crowd cheered for Wells on every pitch. "I was hoping

Yankees catcher Jorge Posada masterminded the game plan that gave Wells his perfect game. Here Wells enjoys the cheers of the fans as his teammates carry him on their shoulders.

the fans would kind of shush a little bit," Wells admitted in postgame interviews. "They were making me nervous out there. I'd run out there and they'd start screaming and yelling. It was great, though."

In all of major league history, only 14 pitchers before Wells had thrown a perfect game. After the last out, a harmless fly to right field by Pat Meares, Wells jabbed his fist in the air, shouting for joy. Teammates heaved the hefty hurler to their shoulders, carrying him from the field. The fans wouldn't allow Wells to leave, cheering until he returned to the field for another bow.

Never before had a Yankee pitched a perfect regular-season game. The last time—the only time—Yankee Stadium hosted a perfect game was in 1956, when New York's Don Larsen no-hit the Brooklyn Dodgers in Game Six of the World Series.

According to catcher Posada, all Wells could say after the last magical out was, "'Jorge, this is great.' He must have said it six times!"

Later, Wells managed to tell countless reporters, "This hasn't all sunk in yet. It's a dream come true." But in the Yankees game plan, it was only one brick needed to pave the way on the road to the World Series.

> David Wells wasn't the only pitcher ever to shock the Twins with perfection. On May 8, 1968, Oakland's Jim "Catfish" Hunter threw a perfect game against Minnesota. Coincidentally, the Yankees signed the future Hall of Famer as a free agent in 1975.

2 MINDING THE MINORS

If a player's ability hasn't blossomed yet, team officials will try to decide whether he needs to be "farmed out." Like the name implies, the "farm system"—baseball's nickname for the minor leagues—is a place where players can grow in experience and skills.

The idea of minor leagues is nearly as old as baseball itself. In 1877 when professional baseball was about 10 years old, the International Association was formed in Pittsburgh. The teams weren't as good as major league teams, and they didn't pay players as much. Still their players could make some money while learning and practicing skills needed to succeed in the major leagues.

Minor league teams used to be graded almost like school classes. Players on a Class D team weren't flunking but were probably just starting their careers. A Class D player would try to move up to C, B, then A. Graduation meant making the majors. A graduating player's team would make some much-needed money by "selling" his contract to the majors.

In 1926 Branch Rickey, then general manager of the St. Louis Cardinals, created the first farm "system." He made a deal with certain minor league teams: The Cardinals would pay the minor leaguers' salaries; in turn, the players would "belong" to St. Louis. In this way, the Cardinals could sign promising young players at lower costs, before any other teams could get them. Pleased with the results, St. Louis bought and juggled prospects from 27 different minor league teams in the 1920s.

Today's teams work with fewer farm clubs. Minors are now classified as rookie league, A, AA, and AAA. Each big-league club has a working agreement with at least three specific minor league teams, at different levels. The major league "parent club" still pays all the players, which is why teams like the Triple-A Iowa Cubs in Des Moines

For years, minor leagues have traditionally served as training grounds for major league baseball players. The minor league shown here is the 1929 Dallas, Texas, league.

don't have a lot of say in who is on their team. If the parent team in Chicago needs a hitter or pitcher, they'll "call up" players from Triple-A, even if Iowa needs those players to clinch a league division.

Players often don't advance the way they would like to in the minors. Some try a different kind of league. Cecil Fielder began as a substitute with the 1985 Toronto Blue Jays. In four seasons of part-time play, Fielder couldn't win a regular position. So he chose to leave the majors, signing a deal to play professionally in Japan in 1989. The next year, other teams laughed when the Detroit Tigers signed Fielder to a two-year contract. He was unproven, they said, from unfamiliar leagues. Fielder quieted critics by slugging 51 homers and batting in 132 runs, leading the majors in his first year back.

DETOURING TO THE MAJORS

Players have still other choices. In the United States, independent leagues such as the Northwest League are made up of teams with no major league ties. Today's independents no longer sell their talent to big teams with big money, just to fans buying tickets. These teams are an alternative for players and fans alike. For example, Philadelphia's 1997 first-round draft pick, J.D. Drew, didn't like the money the Phillies offered. So he joined the Northern League's St. Paul Saints, playing for that team in 1997 and part of 1998, until he was offered a job with the St. Louis Cardinals. A league of overlooked players had given him the stage to show his skills.

· · · · · · · · · · · · · · · · · ·

Hall of Famer Al Kaline's career began with the 1954 Tigers, following his high-school graduation. Kaline's 22-year career with Detroit came without a day of minor league experience.

Likewise, when veteran Darryl Strawberry was released (a polite word for fired) following drug problems, he headed to the same minor league club. St. Paul helped him prove his game and health were better, and the Yankees gave him another chance. In both cases, fans were thrilled with their hometown team, filling the stadium at every game, year after year.

GROWING OTHER TALENTS

The minor leagues do more than train future players. Umpires start in the minors, too. So do future managers. For no matter how long a man had played in the majors, the main reason that he would get a job leading a big-league team is that he showed managerial skills in the mi-

Darryl Strawberry signs autographs for St. Paul Saints fans in 1996.

nors. Often, managers have at least one season's experience heading teams at each minor league level.

The manager may be assisted by one or two coaches, depending on the level of minors and the budget provided by the major league team. The faculty may also feature roving instructors. Traveling from one minor league level to another, a roving instructor is a teaching specialist in one area of the game, such as baserunning or defense. These teachers could advance to the better-paying majors by showing top work in the minors.

For all minor leaguers, the most promising time of the season comes on September 1. That's the date when major league rosters can expand from 25 to 40 players. A major league team can promote players from

Good things come to those who wait. Shane Spencer, who hit a record 10 home runs in his first 70 at-bats with the 1998 Yankees, spent his first eight seasons in the minors.

any level of the minors. But the agreement between the players' union and the club owners states that a new player can be moved between the majors and minors for only three seasons. Each season is an "option." A player can be moved from minors to majors and back endlessly for those three years. But when the player is "out of options," the player can refuse a demotion and get his "free agency," the right to sign a contract with any other team.

Less than 10 out of 100 minor leaguers ever play a day in the majors. But think of how many never sign a professional contract, never even get close to the dream of becoming a big leaguer. Major league managers, like farmers who plant a variety of crops, realize that their farm systems should produce something. Knowing when those seeds of greatness will grow is the most uncertain part of any game plan.

MANAGERS AND MORE 3

Fans sometimes shout—or at least talk to themselves—when their favorite team is losing.

"Take that pitcher out! His arm is shot for today. Man, if I were in charge. . . ."

Atlanta Braves owner Ted Turner decided to take charge when his team suffered a 16-game losing streak in 1977. Turner donned a uniform and called himself manager, even though coach Vern Benson handled the game plan. The stunt backfired: Not only did the team lose—again—but the Commissioner of Baseball quickly ruled that owners couldn't manage, too!

Like Turner, owners of struggling teams often start making changes at the top. A different leader may bring a new team spirit to a losing organization, or have a game plan that makes better use of players.

Teams sometimes take drastic action to get new managers. The Pittsburgh Pirates wanted to hire Oakland A's manager Chuck Tanner for their 1977 season, but the A's still had Tanner under contract. Pittsburgh traded $100,000 and catcher Manny Sanguillen for the rights to hire the manager.

An earlier midseason shocker had taken place on August 10, 1960. The Detroit Tigers, unhappy with skipper Joe Gordon, and the Cleveland Indians, disappointed in Jimmy Dykes, found an unprecedented solution—they traded managers!

Not surprisingly, teams often hire new managers who have recently been fired by other teams. While their old teams may have blamed the men for losing records, new teams may be more open-minded, looking deeper to see if a manager's old team had any talent to win with.

Good managers may not always choose different rosters, but they always try different ideas. For example, most coaches want to start a game with a bang. Their best batters go first, their worst batters last. That's why some reporters in 1998 thought that St. Louis skipper Tony LaRussa was insulting shortstop Royce Clayton by batting him last. But LaRussa pointed out that, after the last batter, the first hitters come back. A *better* hitter—like Clayton— might get on base more often, helping top-of-the-order sluggers create more runs. And LaRussa's third-spot batter that year was Mark McGwire, who was chasing the single-season home-run record.

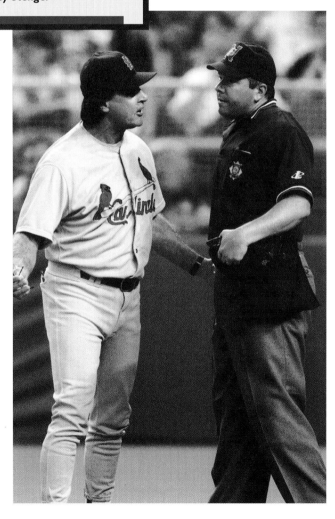

St. Louis Cardinals manager Tony LaRussa disputes a call by umpire Sam Holbrook during a March 1998 game against the Houston Astros.

Makes sense. Even so, few managers have challenged tradition since Bobby Bragan, manager of the 1956 Pirates, launched this game plan by batting a pitcher seventh.

PUZZLED BY POOR-HITTING PITCHERS

National League managers like LaRussa may envy the American League's "designated hitter" rule: Pitchers don't bat; a teammate bats for them. National League game plans become more complex because pitchers must bat for themselves.

For example, when a manager removes a pitcher, he may replace a fielder at the same time. If the "double switch" is made in the middle of an inning, the manager can then decide which replacement bats where in the order. Suppose the ninth-place batter—usually the pitcher—will bat first the next inning. If the manager also replaces the fielder who bats seventh, the two new players can switch spots in the order. That means the pitcher could work an extra inning before having to bat. Since pitchers seldom hit as well as position players, managers who juggle their lineups in this way hope to strengthen their offense.

Managers need leadership skills, not only the ability to handle players but their personalities as well. Only 9 players can start at once, though 25 are on the team. Which players will do best in certain game situations? Will players who don't start remain happy and hardworking until they get a chance? What other factors influence attitudes? For example, the media are part of baseball's world. The press praised manager "Sparky" Anderson for winning three World Championships, his last with the 1984 Tigers. But because Anderson was eager to remove starting pitchers early in games, the media dubbed him "Captain Hook." If Sparky's team had trusted him before, the reporters might have given them doubts.

Another mark of good leadership is knowing when—and whom—to ask for help. Although manager Joe Torre got most of the credit when his 1998 World Champion Yankees set an AL record with 114 wins in the regular season, he depended on bench coach Don Zimmer, a man with nearly a half-century of experience in pro baseball. Bench (or "dugout") coaches are often the wise old owls of baseball. They may be much older than the manager, with more years of experience playing or coaching in the minors and majors.

Try looking up the playing records of successful managers or coaches. Some, like Torre or Cleveland's Mike Hargrove, enjoyed several all-star seasons—but most did not. This strikes some fans as odd. One popular explanation is that a part-time player or longtime minor leaguer may have tried many positions, doing whatever was needed to

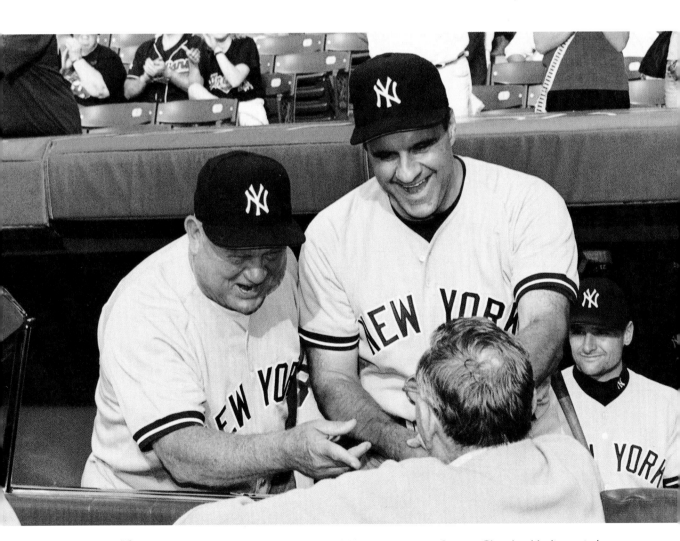

N.Y. Yankees manager Joe Torre (right) and Don Zimmer greet former Cleveland Indians pitching great Bob Lemon. Lemon managed the Yankees in the late 1970s and 1980s.

get into games. Such players also spend more time out of games than stars do—sitting, watching, and learning.

HIRED TO BE FIRED

Billy Martin was a steady but unspectacular player who went on to become a high-profile and often-fired skipper. He left and rejoined the Yankees in four different seasons (1975–1979, 1983, 1985, then 1988). Why would the team keep hiring him back? Because an experienced manager is hard to find. Martin had 20 years experience as a player, scout, and minor league manager before his first job leading the 1969 Minnesota Twins. Martin knew the inner workings of baseball: what to expect from fans, umpires, and the media, and how to produce winning teams.

Could you outmanage a manager? On Aug. 24, 1951, St. Louis Browns owner Bill Veeck let his crowd of 1,115 fans try. Fans held two signs, one "yes" and one "no." Everyone voted on plays such as "should we warm up a new pitcher?" In the end, the fans and Browns beat the Philadelphia Athletics, 5–3.

Experience comes in many forms. Larry Dierker was a steady but unspectacular pitcher on the Houston Astros for 14 years. After his playing days, Dierker became even better known for his honest, thoughtful game commentaries during TV and radio broadcasts of Astros games. The team owners thought that his opinions made sense, and in 1997 gave him the skipper's seat over candidates with years of managerial experience.

How long Dierker stays is anybody's guess. Bobby Bragan, who managed three different teams over seven years, summed up the life of a manager in four words: "Hired to be fired." Walter "Smokey" Alston, who managed the Los Angeles Dodgers, was hired for only one season at a time—for 23 years!

What was Alston's secret to staying hired? "Be your own self," he said. "If you know yourself, you'll know your players." Being a manager is being a teacher, cheerleader, parent, and mastermind for a family of 25 players. Knowing their own style and game plan is the way managers win their games and keep jobs.

4 THE SWEETEST SWING

Think of it. A hitting star may fail in two of every three trips to the plate. Still, if that player gets one hit in every three tries, he has a .333 batting average—and a likely chance of stardom.

Great hitters don't just practice—they do homework! Tony Gwynn of the San Diego Padres had won eight batting titles prior to 1998. Gwynn was noted for carrying his own VCR during Padres road trips, to review his past performances against pitchers he was about to face.

A left-handed hitter, Gwynn excelled at hitting balls where they were pitched. He would normally pull inside deliveries to right field and just punch outside pitches to left field. But strikeouts happen, even with Gwynn's amazing bat control. Surprisingly, Gwynn felt worst when he went down swinging. "If you get caught looking," he'd tell reporters, "you can tell yourself, 'If I had swung, I would have hit it.'"

In more than one season, Gwynn came close to becoming the first .400 hitter since Ted Williams of the Boston Red Sox batted .406 in 1941. Williams was one of the first hitters to speak about the importance of wrists in hitting. He explained that a hard, accurate swing started with quick wrist action.

Nicknamed "Thumper" and "Teddy Ballgame," Williams broke into the majors in 1939. His earliest roommates talked about how Williams, still wearing pajamas, would awaken everyone by standing in front of hotel-room mirrors practicing his swing. Soon his control at bat was producing an amazing ratio of three walks for every strikeout. Legends arose about his perfect eyesight. One reporter claimed that Williams could read a music record's label while it was spinning on the turntable at 78 revolutions per minute.

THE SCIENCE OF SPORT

Nearly a decade after he retired, Williams co-authored *The Science of Hitting* with John Underwood. The 1971 book was adored by fans. In this tell-all textbook, Williams documented his hitting zones. He divided his

Legendary slugger Ted Williams of the Boston Red Sox hit his 499th career home run in a game against the Detroit Tigers on June 16, 1960.

strike zone with baseballs, 11 balls high and 7 wide. The 77 balls were colored to denote pitches in different locations. Williams showed the importance of knowing your personal strengths by estimating what average he would hit for each pitch. He guessed that he would hit .230 against low outside strikes. For pitches in his "happy zone," waist-high across the plate, Williams bet he would hit .400.

Williams focused on average, on putting the ball into play so runners have a chance to score. How far the ball travels isn't as important as simply getting a hit.

Hitters seek any boost they can get at bat. Around 1960, Yankee catcher Elston Howard found a legal way to make his bat seem lighter. He created a doughnut-shaped metal weight to slip over the bat barrel while taking practice swings in the on-deck circle. When he removed the doughnut to take his turn at bat, the unweighted bat seemed magically easier to wield.

Some bats seem lighter because they have been "doctored." The barrel of a doctored bat may be hollow, or filled with cork, then concealed. A ball hit with a corked bat will travel farther. But, just like a blown-out eggshell, doctored bats become more fragile. In the 1990s Chris Sabo and Wilton Guerrero were but two players whose bats broke at the plate to reveal tampering. Players face fines and suspensions for such wrongdoing.

Other rules are more difficult to enforce. George Brett of the Kansas City Royals thought he slugged a game-winning homer against the Yankees in 1983. But New York manager Billy Martin told umpires that Brett had broken the rules. Pine tar, a sticky black goo meant to help hitters grip the bat tighter, is legal within limits. Martin protested that Brett had smeared tar too far up his bat's handle. Brett was called out, his homer erased, and the Yankees won—until the Royals protested that, according to the rules, only Brett's bat could be removed, *not his homer*. That meant the Yankees had a half-inning coming, which was played the following month. Kansas City won, after all.

The simplest legal way to make a bat feel better is to change bats. Switch-hitters, who can bat from either side of the plate, often use different models or brands of bats if batting left- or right-handed.

WHICH WOOD WORKS?

Talk turned to lumber in 1998, when two players raced after the single-season home-run record. What type of bat, reporters wondered, seemed best when swinging for the fences?

Babe Ruth of the New York Yankees used a 36-ounce bat that was 35 inches long when he homered 60 times in 1927. Another Yankee, Roger Maris, broke the Babe's record by one, going deep 61 times in 1961. Maris swung a 33-ounce, 35-inch bat. Chasing Maris's record in 1998, St. Louis Cardinal slugger Mark McGwire would use only the Rawlings brand he had favored during his entire career. Sammy Sosa of the Chicago Cubs, neck-and-neck with McGwire in 1998's home-run derby, made the science of

bat selection simple. His numerous blasts were achieved with an assortment of bats made by two different companies. Like old-time players, Sosa grabbed the stick that felt best for him that game.

Although players may use similar bats, few choose similar stances. There are countless choices of how to stand in the batter's box. Hall of Famer Joe Morgan adopted the "chicken flap," a reminder to keep his back shoulder high for a smoother swing. Stan Musial, a Cardinals star slugger of the 1940s and

> Tall Ted Williams, who was called the "Splendid Splinter," sought splendid splinters as bats. The president of the Louisville Sluggers bat company once showed Ted Williams six bats. After swinging each, Williams knew which bat weighed just a half-ounce more.

A typical selection of bats used in a 1998 major league game

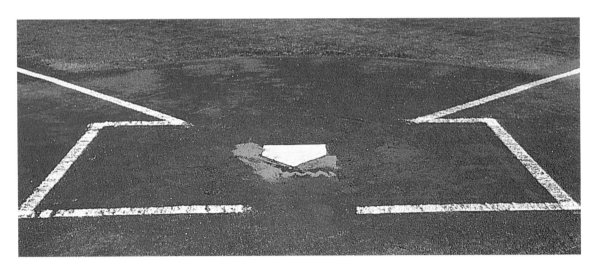

In the layout of a major league baseball field, home plate is centered within a 4- by 6-foot batter's box marked by chalk lines.

> Coaches who tell you not to let the bat hit the ball on the label side may be giving good advice for the wrong reason. The old belief that bats will crack that way isn't true. However, the bat is stronger on the untouched grainy side, meaning that the ball may go farther if you listen to the coach.

1950s, chose a stance that some reporters said looked like a coiled spring, or a snake ready to pounce.

Hitters also think about *where* they stand as they take their stance. With a 4- by 6-foot box chalked out on each side of the plate, it seems as if hitters wouldn't have many choices. But watch how fast those chalk lines around home plate are stomped out at the start of a game. Players standing in the front of the box may hope to reach curves before they break. Other players scoot back, hoping to get an extra peek at fastballs. The rule saying that players hitting outside of the box can be called out is seldom enforced, though umpires sometimes borrow a bat to retrace the box lines.

The hitting game plan changes often, with new techniques and equipment, with every new game. But the oldest, simplest technique—patience, following Ted Williams's command to "get a good pitch to hit"—is still the best game plan of all.

THE RUNNING GAME

5

"First base is nowhere," record-breaking base stealer Lou Brock wrote in his 1976 autobiography, *Stealing Is My Game*. "Second base is probably the safest place on the field. When I steal second, I practically eliminate the double play, and I can score on almost any hit past the infield."

In 1974 the 34-year-old Brock swiped 118 bases. He broke the season standard set in 1962 by Los Angeles Dodger Maury Wills, who had 104 stolen bases in 117 tries. Wills had broken Ty Cobb's record of 96, which had stood since 1915. Fans wonder how long it will take to break the current season record of 130 by career leader Rickey Henderson. Henderson in 1994 became the first speedster to surpass 1,000 stolen bases, and he did it all with head-first slides.

Like Brock, Henderson wrote a book. It begins, "Yes, I am a hot dog." Habitual base stealers can seem like show-offs. But base stealing is a game plan for more than personal glory. Stealing helps a team by getting runs, even without hits.

Speed helps when stealing bases, but it's not always needed. In fact, being known as cement-footed can baffle opponents even more. A favorite play that managers use for mediocre runners is the double steal. With a speedster on third base and a slowpoke on first, a manager sends the slower man first. The fielders suspect the double steal and, like dogs smelling meat, often bite at the temptation. The chase is

Speedy Ricky Henderson of the Oakland A's steals second base in this June 1995 photo.

on to nab the runner streaking home. Meanwhile, the runner on first base tiptoes safely to second, credited with a stolen base.

Batters can help base stealers, too. Those who stand deeper in the box may not have as much reaction time when swinging, but they block the catcher's view and give him less room to stop base thefts. Likewise, batters who "take" some pitches—don't swing at them—give runners more opportunities to steal.

PITCHERS VERSUS RUNNERS

Most baseball fans agree that it's the pitcher's job to "hold" runners, keep them from stealing bases. A pitcher praised for a strong pickoff move is probably a lefty. Left-handed pitchers face first base as they prepare to throw. Baffled base-runners don't know whether the hurler is headed for a pitch or a pickoff.

But runners have left and right tricks up their sleeves, too. Base stealer Brock explained that being left-footed, he led with that foot, giving him shorter leads off the bag. Short leads made him harder to pick off, and his left-footed starts gave him quicker acceleration to second base.

Stealers like Brock can cause pitchers to "balk." That occurs when a pitcher breaks the rules by interrupting his windup to try a pickoff, or stands on the pitching rubber while making a pickoff throw.

The "pitchout" is a game plan the manager or catcher might use if a steal is suspected. Here, the pitcher purposely delivers a ball several feet outside the plate. The catcher, leaping to his feet, has a head start in cutting down a base stealer.

Managers may give the "green light" for their best runners to steal at any time. But the running game is more than stealing bases. First- and third-base coaches play a vital role in keeping teams on the move. Knowing that the batter will make contact, no matter what, an infield coach may "start the runner" from first toward second. Even a slow runner has enough of a start to make a double play impossible. The only sure out remains the batter. And if the batter's grounder turns into a hit, a runner on the move could wind up at third base on a single.

Winning the last game of the 1946 World Series, Enos Slaughter of the St. Louis Cardinals became legendary for his "mad dash." Running with the pitch, he scored from first on a double by Harry Walker. The opposing shortstop was so surprised that he hesitated, and Slaughter slid in under the tag.

The manager of a minor league team often doubles as the third-base coach. Often called the team's "traffic cop," the third-base coach has an excellent view of all the action, unlike a runner who may have his back to the fielder with the ball. Yet players sometimes "run

Batters who hit singles need to run with care. Runners who pass first base into foul territory can't be tagged out. However, once the runner turns toward second base, the tag counts.

through a stop sign" and try to advance from third to home, despite the warning signals of the third-base coach.

Good coaches can get runners from second to third by studying the twists in a game. A runner who is sacrifice-bunted from first base to second needs to watch the coach. If the bunt went to a charging third baseman, is any fielder still guarding third? Going from second to third can be like a free pass when no fielder is there to tag the runner.

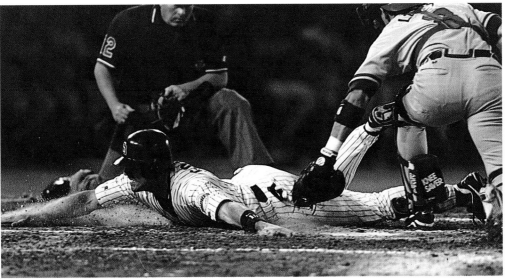

There are several ways to slide into base. The top photo shows Toronto Blue Jays Felipe Crespo in a typical leg-first slide. The bottom photo shows San Diego Padres Chris Gomez in a headfirst slide.

THE SAFE SLIDE

Knowing how to reach a base takes more than speed. If a runner knows the ball may be only a split-second away, he may try a "hook" or "fade-away" slide. Instead of heading straight into the base, the runner will keep just one hand or toe in the baseline to tag with. If a throw is coming from the outfield to second, a runner should hook-slide to the infield side of the base. The game plan? Give a fielder as small a target as possible to tag.

Stopping the fadeaway can be difficult—for the runner. The momentum of the slide often carries a runner right past the bag. And if a runner is not touching the base, he can be tagged out. Fielders who don't give up could tag out a safe runner who slides past the bag.

Runners on first and second base lead off in the baseline. However, the runner on third should stay in foul territory. Why? The runner off third in fair ground is out when hit by a batted ball.

In a huge ballpark where home runs are difficult, or when a team has few sluggers, players must run for their wins. Quickness counts in these game plans—quick feet and quick wits.

6 FIELDING QUESTIONS

Today's major league teams often favor fielders with the "right" stuff.

Traditional baseball wisdom holds that left-handers shouldn't play second base, shortstop, or third base. With his glove on his right hand, a lefty would need to pivot his entire body to get an accurate throw to first base—and every second counts when trying to turn hits into groundouts.

At catcher, right-handers are seen to have an advantage, too. Because baseball began with more right-handed hitters, right-throwing catchers didn't have a batter in their way when throwing to any of the bases. In fact, left-handed catchers have been so rare that finding a mitt can be impossible. When the notable lefty pitcher Sandy Koufax occasionally helped fellow Dodger pitchers warm up before games, he would reshape a right-handed catcher's mitt, designed to be worn on the left hand, so it would fit his right hand.

First base is the only infield position where left-handedness brings a bonus. With the mitt on the right hand, lefties have a closer, simpler reach in tagging out runners during pickoff plays. And a left-handed first baseman doesn't have to pivot when throwing to second or third base.

Shortstop Ozzie Smith was dubbed "The Wizard" during 15 years with the St. Louis Cardinals. His skill looked like magic because he had so much fun. But Smith studied field and game conditions, knowing what to expect whether he was playing on bouncy artificial turf, high (and slow) grass, or a dry, fast infield. He knew the opposing hitters, and which pitches they favored from each Cardinal pitcher. Most of all, Smith charged as many grounders as possible. Running in on the ball assured that he would have extra time to make a shorter, easier throw. Smith proved the old baseball saying: "Play the ball. Don't let the ball play you."

Smith, considered one of the best infielders ever, committed few errors. But excellent fielders sometimes make many errors. It's not just because the official scorers are really reporters who work in the team's home city. (Some fans are sure scorers are nicer to the home team!) Less talented fielders may make few errors because baseball rules allow for individual abilities.

Every infielder can be described in terms of "range"(that is, how much ground he can cover to his left or right). Also, baseball rules state that "slow handling of the ball which does not involve mechanical misplay shall not be construed as an error." In other words, infielders who don't risk throwing on a close play cannot be charged with an error. However, a fielder with confidence in his arm will try to throw out anyone. Branch Rickey, the famed general manager of the Brooklyn Dodgers, called such plays "errors of enthusiasm."

The best infielders are smart and patient. They are praised for their "soft hands." They don't stab at the ball but treat oncoming grounders like airborne eggs. Gentle fielding can be especially difficult for a pitcher who has just thrown to the plate. He has to recover quickly from his throw, trying not to drift to either side of the mound, and be instantly ready to stop any grounders up the middle.

Al Campanis lasted less than a year catching in the big leagues. But as general manager of the Dodgers in the 1970s, he had a brainstorm about catching. "I was driving home from Dodger Stadium, when I saw some workmen on the highway. It was night and the men wore orange reflective jackets." Immediately, Campanis thought to use that same orange around the edge of a mitt, making the "target mitt." The idea caught on.

St. Louis Cardinals Ozzie Smith displays some of the athletic ability that made him an outstanding shortstop as he leaps for a wild pitch.

FIELDING PITCHERS

Covering first is another difficult fielding play for pitchers. If the first baseman needs to range far toward second base for a grounder, the pitcher needs to be ready to cover first base at once. The first baseman will underhand a throw, which the pitcher must catch cleanly while stepping on the bag for the out and avoiding a collision with the runner.

Catchers risk more collisions than any other players. "Blocking the plate" is a dangerous part of their job. With this fielding method, the catcher stands in the third-base line, awaiting a throw. The runner is forced to slide around—or through—the catcher, slowing down his effort to score. Collisions resulting from this play are just one reason injuries are common among catchers. Foul balls and flying bats cause so many finger cuts, bruises, and breaks that Chicago Cubs catcher Randy Hundley in the 1960s popularized one-handed catching, tucking his throwing hand behind his back.

ROAMING THE OUTFIELD

Outfielders seem to need more speed than their infielding teammates, with all the ground they have to cover. And speed does help: Slow runners are often stunned when a grounder that should have been a single is charged by an outfielder and whipped to first base for the out. But even fly balls require special care. A misplayed fly can cost big, creating an inside-the-park home run. That's why top 1990s flyhawkers like Kenny Lofton gained fame for their leaping abilities. They could jump higher than the outfield wall, reaching above the fence top to snare possible home runs with their gloves.

Before 1948, outfield walls terrorized outfielders. Outfielders who kept their eyes on the ball often got a high-impact surprise from the wall. Today, a "warning track" made of cinders

. . . .
Playing defense, you'd be lucky to get a "snow cone." It's not a snack, it's a baseball term for the ball sticking out of the top of the glove. The ball is on the glove fingertips, ready to squirt out the top after a shaky catch. For either kind of snow cone, the rule is, "Hold on!"

N.Y. Yankees right fielder Paul O'Neill goes high on the wall to make a spectacular run-saving catch in the second game of the 1998 World Series.

or crushed rock forms a strip between the outfield grass and the wall. An outfielder can see, and feel with his feet, the signal that the wall is coming. Additionally, big-league stadiums now feature padded walls to protect against injury.

When a hit bounces off the outfield wall, an infielder sprints into the outfield. The outfielder is expected to "hit" this "cutoff man," with the infielder who left his position relaying the throw. For example, if the first baseman standing near the mound sees that the runner on second is almost home anyway, he can "cut off" the well-aimed throw from the outfielder and nab the hitter who is almost at second. An overeager outfielder who tries to throw out runners without infield help can allow other runners to advance.

Baseball awards Gold Gloves yearly to the best fielders. The awards, given since 1957, are now voted on by managers and coaches (who may not choose players on their own teams). But a top fielding percentage, even fewest errors in the league, won't guarantee the award. What earns the most votes is how a player's glove work helped his team.

The award is well named. If you ask any manager or pitcher who has won a close game due to strong defense, he will tell you that good fielders are worth their weight in gold.

7 ON THE MOUND

Athletes and fans alike disagree as to which matters most, talent or knowledge. But great pitchers understand that while physical ability may lessen with time or injury, there is no end to polishing knowledge and attitude.

Atlanta Braves ace Greg Maddux, winner of four Cy Young awards (for best pitcher of the year) prior to 1998, would usually sit on the bench next to hitting coach Clarence Jones between innings. "Sometimes when you sit next to other players, you get distracted and end up paying attention to something besides the game," Maddux told reporters. He wanted to soak up tips that the coach dished out to batters. Maddux wanted to think like a batter, like the foes he would face in future innings. Other Braves pitchers claimed that Maddux watched opposing players so carefully, he would even notice batters *on deck* and anticipate how they might bat.

Knowing which pitches a batter hates can help a hurler, but only if he can throw those pitches well. Health is a factor. When Kevin Tapani began 1998 with the Chicago Cubs, he no longer could throw his split-fingered fastball. The skin between his index and middle fingers had ripped and, after healing, didn't allow him to spread his fingers far enough for a split-fingered grip.

Then again, a new pitch can revive a sagging career. A pitcher can't throw the same specialty pitch forever, just because he knows the delivery. Steve Sparks bounced around the minors for more than three years until he learned the art of the effortless knuckleball. The knuckler is thrown without any rotation, which can make the pitch harder to swat than a crazed butterfly. The batters don't know which way to expect the pitch to move. That's why the knuckleball was Sparks's ticket to the majors. In fact, pitchers like Hall of Famers Phil Niekro and Hoyt Wilhelm stayed active until their late 40s by lobbing this soft, deceptive pitch.

Oakland A's pitcher Tom Candiotti shows the grip for a knuckleball.

SLOW BUT STEADY

Pitching for the Baltimore Orioles and Boston Red Sox in the 1980s, Mike Boddicker won more than 100 games. He was a leading "junkball" pitcher, one whose many off-speed pitches were described as slow, slower, and slowest. In fact, Baltimore teammates said Boddicker's best pitch was a "foshball," which they said looked like a forkball crossed with a dead fish.

Hall of Famer Rod Carew was one of many hitters frustrated by Boddicker. "I take better stuff out to the garbage every night!" he said, angry at being called out on such slow stuff. Like many hitters, Carew tried to time his swing while looking for a specific pitch. A good junkballer can confuse a batter's timing for days after a tough game.

Bob Feller, known as "Bullet Bob," "Rapid Robert," or "the Heater from Van Meter" (his Iowa hometown), began pitching with the Cleveland Indians as a teenager in 1936. In 1998 he made baseball news by disagreeing with team doctors who diagnosed two Indians hurlers with "dead arms," arms that simply needed rest. Dead arms? "Dead brain cells are more like it!" Feller told reporters.

Coaches will look at many clues to see how a pitcher's arm is and decide if he can continue. One overlooked indication is foul balls. When hitters are fouling pitches straight back behind home plate, they are closer than ever to connecting. Fouls in the left- or right-field seats may be near homers, but the batters are still too early or late in timing their swings.

> Not only were Pittsburgh's Kent Tekulve and Kansas City's Dan Quisenberry top relievers in the 1980s, but they were keepers of a lost art. Both mastered the whiplike, near-underhand motion of "submarine" pitching.

On the other hand, coaches will ask if the pitcher is too closely on target. That is, is the pitcher failing to work the corners of the plate? Are breaking pitches going flat, "hanging" up in the high, easy-to-hit part of the strike zone? If so, it may be time for a change.

Nolan Ryan found the strike zone a record number of times in his 27 seasons. The fastballer struck out a history-making 5,714 batters. Along with a record 7 no-hitters, Ryan earned 324 wins. He was elected to the Hall of Fame in 1999, his first year of eligibility. Of 497 ballots cast by the Baseball Writers Association of America, only 6 didn't have votes for the Texas starter. Ignoring the 98.7 percent of votes for Ryan, his few critics pointed out his 292 losses.

STOPPING FOR THE STARTER

A starter is asked to do one job: Pitch as many innings as possible. Relievers come with many different assignments.

A young Bob Feller winds up to throw a pitch in 1940. This outstanding pitcher was elected to the Hall of Fame in 1962.

> When pitchers talk about gripping a baseball across, or with, the laces, they don't have time to stop and count what they are squeezing. A baseball has 108 stitches.

Fans hear most about the "closer," the relief ace whose outings seldom last more than one inning. Managers like to use this reliever only to preserve a lead, to work the final inning and seal a victory.

The bullpen men called "long" or "middle" relievers are needed only when the starter is removed from the game in the first or second inning. These early relievers are asked to keep the score close and to pitch as many innings as possible. A "setup" reliever will be called to hold the score in late innings, setting up the closer's entry.

A bullpen trend in the 1990s was keeping one-batter specialists. A reliever, a left- or right-hander, would be asked to get just one out. Defensive managers believe in choosing a pitcher who throws from the same side the hitter bats from because it is harder to see someone pitching from the same side.

PITCHING A FIT

One of the most unusual pitching game plans came from Al Hrabosky, a St. Louis Cardinals relief pitcher. Nicknamed "the Mad Hungarian," he was the buzz of the 1970s. With the bases empty, the scowling moundsman with the fu manchu moustache would pace behind the mound for a minute of self-hypnosis, visualizing each batter's weakness. He'd mutter to himself, then march back to the pitching rubber. As he slammed the ball into his mitt, fans would roar at Hrabosky's rage.

"I was doing it for myself, not just for the fans," Hrabosky remembered.

Like all the best mound magicians, Hrabosky was looking for a way to see nothing but the catcher's mitt, hear only the smack of the ball hitting leather. Only a pitcher has the chance to turn every hitter into an out. No wonder the game plans of pitchers are often the most compelling and complex.

SECRET WEAPONS

Reporters love to ask managers how to beat an upcoming team.

"If I knew," the manager often replies, "why would I tell you?"

Sure, he may be a little annoyed at journalists who think he's a fortune-teller. But managers know that their opponents want as much information as possible before a game—and they will watch the media to get it.

Watching pregame warm-ups is another way to get clues. To help players adjust to the field, a coach uses a thick-headed, far-hitting "fungo" bat to hit grounders and fly balls to fielders. Opponents watching the warm-ups get clues about which players may be injured or are not having good days or have the best throwing arms. Rivals can even get clues about how the field plays.

Groundskeepers prepare the field to please the home team. High infield grass can help aging or injured fielders reach more grounders. Mud or sand around the sliding areas near the bases can slow down hits, deaden bunts, and hinder base stealing. True, these would be disadvantages for both teams. But if the opponents have more base stealers and sluggers, field grooming may be worth it.

More clues come from the team's on-field stretching with strength and conditioning coaches. But some clues stay in the clubhouse, where trainers tape bruised, tired muscles to prevent further injury, or give massages to help loosen aching muscles.

Groundskeepers have prepared Coors Field in Denver to the specifications of the home team, the Rockies.

A rare advantage comes when a player has joined a new team and is about to face his old squad. He will be asked to tell which plays his former manager and teammates favored. A competitor can be loyal to only one team at a time.

Often, teams hire former players who are no longer active on-field. These "advance scouts" travel to see upcoming rivals and study possible challenges, such as how certain pitchers are throwing, or the pitches that leading batters like best. Casey Stengel, manager of the Yankees from 1949 to 1960, is often credited with creating this game plan.

CATCHING THE CATCHER

But game plans change with the circumstances of the game. That is why some hitters peek at the catcher's glove before the pitch, for a hint to where the throw might be placed. Some batters get help from team-

In 1976, Dodger catcher Steve Yeager invented the "billy goat" throat protector, a hinged shoehorn-sized shield that hung below his catcher's mask. It is named after the "beard" that hangs below a billy goat's chin. Yeager had been injured when splinters from a shattered bat pierced his throat when he was waiting to hit. He needed extra protection to catch with a wounded neck. But other catchers, who had taken foul tips under their masks, started using his invention, too. So have umpires.

mates on base, who watch the catcher and motion if the catcher's glove is inside or outside. Some runners even try to guess the pitch signals.

Since catchers "call," or signal, for certain pitches, they meet with pitchers before a game to discuss their rivals' hitting tendencies. Entire teams frequently study videos of upcoming opponents, providing a close-up, freeze-framed look at what they have been doing right or wrong. Most teams have video coordinators to record their own mistakes and successes.

Pitching coaches often use stopwatches during games, to clock the time between pitches, or how long it takes a pitcher to release the ball. These times tell if the pitcher is rushing or getting tired. So does the speed of each pitch, as clocked by radar detectors, much like those that police use to detect speeding drivers. Made by various companies, most of these machines are still called "JUGS guns," after the Oregon company that sold some of the first devices to teams.

In 1974, professional baseball started the Major League Scouting Bureau. Reports are shared among all 30 teams, because the bureau is funded by Major League Baseball. But teams still want their own information. "Cross-checkers" are employed by each team. They are sent out across the country to double-check good reports from area scouts.

Professional scouts use radar guns at a high-school baseball game to clock local pitchers.

One of the first ways used to measure a player's fastball before the radar gun was to have him throw beside a speeding motorcycle rider. The cycle had a speedometer, which could estimate how fast the ball had traveled.

When a pitcher will be starting the following game, he must "keep the chart" for the current game. As he writes down every pitch to every hitter, he can see which pitches are working, or failing, against the batters he will see the next day. The pitching coach may also check the charts to see how well the current hurler is throwing.

These charts are often made on a clipboard, but laptop computers are found in dugouts, too. If the rival team has chosen a pinch hitter, or the current pitcher is slowing down, the coaching staff may access computer data to see which pitchers on their staff have done the best against upcoming batters. Next, the pitching coach calls the bullpen coach on a special field telephone. Certain pitchers are asked to warm up. Soon the bullpen coach calls back to the dugout to say which pitchers seem most ready to enter the game.

Even the weather can guide managers in choosing a game plan. For example, a pitcher with a strong sinker or split-fingered fastball would be a good choice for a windy day. His pitches more often turn into grounders, with fewer worries about windblown home runs.

GETTING A LIFT FROM A SHIFT

Outfielders are known to "shade" some hitters during a game. A right-handed swinger dubbed an "opposite field" hitter will drive more pitches to right field, making fielders adjust accordingly.

In 1946, Lou Boudreau was the starting shortstop and manager of the Cleveland Indians. To stop Boston's Ted Williams from piling up hit upon hit, the Indians created the "Williams Shift." Williams was a "pull" hitter, a lefty swinger who drove almost every hit to right field. The Indians moved all their fielders to the right side of the diamond, leaving a hole by third base. But Williams refused to punch soft hits into the unguarded territory.

Williams and the Indians each thought they knew what to expect. So did Cincinnati Reds catcher Johnny Bench in Game 3 of the 1972 World Series. Bench had a full count against Oakland A's pitcher Rollie Fingers—but first base was unoccupied. Instead of risking a big hit, Fingers could walk Bench to set up a double play. Oakland catcher Gene Tenace stood and extended his hand, signaling that the ball should be thrown wide for an intentional walk.

A veteran Cincinnati catcher, Bench knew what that signal meant. He relaxed his stance, loosened his grip on the bat, and waited for the "free pass" Tenace had signaled for. Suddenly, Tenace squatted again behind the plate, catching the third-strike pitch streaking past the unprepared hitter.

Knowing the other team is the key to a surprising, successful strategy. Before the first pitch is thrown, the mind games played could help determine the final score.

9 MARKING HISTORY

On September 8, 1998, baseball fans worldwide were transfixed by the St. Louis Cardinals, a team with no mathematical shot at postseason play. They were playing the Chicago Cubs, a team fighting for a playoff spot. But even Cubs fans were following the Cardinals.

The Fox network broadcast the Tuesday matchup to more than 100 countries. Radio beamed the game to 200-plus nations.

The world was waiting to hear a record break.

Sammy Sosa of the Cubs was racing Mark McGwire of the Cardinals to erase the single-season home-run mark of Yankees outfielder Roger Maris, who had slammed 61 in 1961. Sosa remained stuck on 58 dingers. Yet he had amazed the world once before. At the end of May when McGwire had 24 homers, Sosa had only 9. A record-setting binge of 20 home runs in June made Sosa a contender.

The drama grew the day before the big broadcast. McGwire, in his 446th plate appearance of the season, sent a 1–1 pitch from Mike Morgan on a 430-foot ride out of Busch Stadium. On his father's 61st birthday, McGwire hit his 61st home run of the season, truly one of the most extraordinary gifts a son ever made for his dad.

The city went wild. Even rival teams cheered. But everyone knew that tying a record wasn't the same as breaking it.

The next day held promise. Tuesdays had been good to McGwire in 1998: 14 of his homers came on that day. But on his first at-bat on Tuesday, September 8, McGwire seemed to forget his game plan. He had a count of three balls and no strikes. The slugger's keen batting eye had already given him a record-setting number of walks that season—a record that pitchers were more willing to help with than the record for home runs. But McGwire knew he had a chance to make history that night. He *wanted* to make history. He bit on an outside pitch and grounded out to shortstop.

His next at-bat wasn't until the fourth inning.

McGwire tried to refocus. He maintained his on-deck routine, not taking any warm-up swings, just staring at starting pitcher Steve Traschel. Then, at 8:18 P.M., McGwire did something he almost never did. He attacked the first pitch, an 88-mile-per-hour sinking fastball, lining it to left field. Various play-by-play announcers remained silent, waiting to see where the ball would land.

The ball sailed only 341 feet, but that was enough. It cleared the wall by some 5 feet, just staying in fair territory. McGwire ran full speed to first base, thinking he had a double. But first-base coach Dave McKay forwarded the umpire's circular hand-waving signal to go around the bases for a home run.

Coach McKay hugged McGwire on his way to second, then shouted for his return. Laughing, McGwire scrambled back to touch first. If "Big Mac" had missed first base, the Cubs could have taken the next ball from the umpire and tagged first base for an out before the next hitter stepped in.

> The 1927 Yankees didn't win 110 games just because of Babe Ruth's 60 homers and 175 RBI. The team's pitchers combined for a 3.20 earned-run average, lowest in the league.

A PIECE OF HISTORY

But with first base safely touched, the homer was part of history. A groundskeeper found the famous ball under the stands. But how could anyone be sure it was McGwire's?

Major League Baseball had been carrying out a secret game plan since McGwire's 59th home run. Baseballs pitched to McGwire were

St. Louis Cardinals slugger Mark McGwire hit his record-breaking 62nd home run of the season during the fourth inning of the game against the Chicago Cubs on September 8, 1998. The Cubs pitcher who gave up the hit was Steve Iraschel.

numbered from 1 to 48 in invisible ink. That way, no one could pretend an ordinary ball was part of history. Under a black light, a "12" appeared on the ball the groundskeeper had found, proving that it was the history maker.

The entire baseball world, it seemed, tried to help with McGwire's game plan. Before the game, officials from the National Baseball Hall of Fame in Cooperstown, New York, visited McGwire with the bat that Maris had used to hit his 61st homer. McGwire held the bat barrel to his heart before the game. "Roger, you're with me," he said.

Roger Maris died of cancer in December 1985 at age 51. But a part of him was with McGwire: His family gathered in St. Louis to cheer for McGwire. After shattering the record, McGwire climbed into the stands to hug one Maris after another.

When McGwire finally returned to the field, a blue flash appeared in the sea of Cardinals crowding around McGwire. Cubs Sammy Sosa ran in from his right-field position to hug his St. Louis opponent.

Shown here is the autographed ball from Mark McGwire's 62nd home run. The ball from his 70th home run sold at auction on January 12, 1999, for a record-breaking $3.05 million, including the commission.

BASEBALL AS USUAL

With the record broken, it was back to baseball as usual. The Cubs still had a chance to win the wild-card play-off spot, and Sosa's long-ball stroke came back to help: Wrigley Field fans saw him go deep twice in two days soon after McGwire's success.

On September 13, 1998, pitcher Bronswell Patrick of the Milwaukee Brewers delivered a no-ball, one-strike fastball that became a fifth-inning footnote to history. Sosa drove the ball more than 480 feet over the left-field fence onto Waveland Avenue. Sosa had tied Maris.

Reliever Eric Plunk opposed Sosa in the bottom of the ninth. In a near-instant replay, Sosa's second homer, number 62, dropped to the same neighborhood street. No officials from Major League Baseball attended. No Maris family members came. No baseballs were marked with secret ink.

But the Wrigley faithful roared, urging Sosa to emerge from the dugout to bow once, twice, three times. He saluted local fans with his famous gesture—pounding his fist to his heart, blowing kisses to his mother overseas, and flashing the "V for victory" sign to honor deceased announcer Harry Caray. Back in the dugout, Sosa looked into a TV camera. A face covered in sweat and tears mouthed the words, "I love you, Mama." She was still back home in San Pedro de Macoris, the Dominican Republic. As a youth, Sosa had shined shoes and sold oranges on the street to help support his family.

Sosa's second home run tied the all-time record and helped push the game into extra innings. The Cubs finally triumphed with Mark Grace's game-winning, 10th-inning homer. Later, Grace jokingly apologized for the hit. By ending the game, he left Sosa on deck, waiting to hit a 63rd homer!

Tied at 62, neither Sosa nor McGwire revealed a game plan for becoming history's home-run king. Sosa repeated his wish to help the Cubs to the playoffs. McGwire maintained that ending the year with a .300 average was most important to him.

"If he's ahead or I'm ahead, I would not have one complaint, one iota," McGwire said. "You know what? All I can do is control what I do."

WHAT RECORDS BRING

Which slugger's game plan was a winner? That depends on the definition of "winner."

On Friday, September 25, Sosa slugged his 66th and final homer in Houston. He led the race—for 45 minutes—before "Big Mac" was back.

McGwire focused on his own efforts. In front of an adoring, supportive St. Louis crowd, he belted five homers in three games off the Montreal Expos.

The season ended with Mc-Gwire rewriting baseball history with 70 home runs. He reached that record by going deep against 65 different hurlers.

Sosa's reply to going homer-less for the last two games of the season was simple: "We're still alive!" he told reporters. His Cubs tied for the league's wild-card spot, and Chicago went on to win a one-game tie-breaker with the San Francisco Giants the next day.

The St. Louis Cardinals had little hope for the playoffs as early as August, and McGwire's achievements couldn't improve their standing. Sosa's 132 runs scored and 158 RBI topped

Chicago Cubs Sammy Sosa doffs his batting helmet to a cheering crowd after hitting his 62nd home run. His blast came in the game against the Milwaukee Brewers on September 13, 1998.

McGwire and everyone else. Second-place "Slammin' Sammy" became part of a top-placed team, while homer king McGwire was left to dream about postseason play.

While two men battled over individual history, only one team seemed ready to rewrite the record books as a group. Without a star-studded lineup, the Yankees became the dictionary definition of teamwork.

Without a single McGwire-like record on their roster, the Yankees supported each other in 1998 with a variety of above-average stats. Bernie Williams won the league batting crown at .339—a nice enough number, but baseball has seen better in years past. In fact, Williams won the title by only two points.

But three other Yankees starters topped .300, too. And, though pitcher David Cone tied for the AL lead with 20 wins, he was only one of six Yankee hurlers with a dozen or more wins.

> The 1998 Yankees didn't win all their home games at Yankee Stadium. Their game on April 13 was canceled when a 500-pound beam crashed into the seats. Two days later, the Yankees rented Shea Stadium, home of the New York Mets, to beat the Angels, 6–3.

It was almost as if the Yankees took turns having good days. A perfect example was David Wells, pitcher of that season's perfect game. In his only Series appearance, Wells took a pounding in Game 1, giving up five runs in seven innings. The Yankees desperately needed power at the bat, and they got it—from players who had dipped below .200 each in postseason play. Yet with the Yankees still trailing 5–2 in the seventh inning, Chuck Knoblauch and Tino Martinez combined for seven runs—a three-run homer for Knoblauch and a grand slam for Martinez.

Game 2 was an easier win. However, Game 3 saw the Yankees behind 3–0 in the seventh inning when Scott Brosius came to the plate. Third baseman Brosius had hit a sickly .203 for Oakland in 1997. But at the Series that night, he led off the seventh inning with a home run. And he wasn't finished. With the Yankees still down 3–2 in the eighth, Brosius smashed a three-run blast that gave New York its third Series win. Brosius batted .471 for the Series, with two home runs and six runs batted in. On his own, he had never been a star, but as a piece in the Yankees puzzle, Brosius was a perfect fit—so perfect he was named the Series MVP.

Without a single individual record setter in their ranks, the Yankees still won a record 125 games throughout 1998 and they needed only four World Series games to get the four victories they needed, "sweeping" the Padres to win it all.

On February 17, 1999, the Yankees refined their game plan to develop a winning team. In a surprise move, they traded David Wells and two other players to the Toronto Blue Jays in exchange for ace pitcher Roger Clemens.

The N.Y. Yankees' game plan may be the longest-lasting. Players who work together can often overcome the single greatest star. It is just such a game plan that makes players into teams, and teams into winners.

N.Y. Yankees celebrate winning the 1998 World Series after defeating the San Diego Padres in the fourth and final game on October 21, 1998. This win was the 24th championship for the Yankees.

GLOSSARY

All-Star Game   not part of the regular season, held yearly since 1933. Representatives from both leagues form two teams. Since 1970, fans have voted for starting players.

assist   credit to a fielder for helping to make an out by touching or throwing a batted ball.

away   1. a game played at the opponent's field. 2. a pitch outside the strike zone, farthest away from a hitter.

backstop   1. the fence behind home plate. 2. nickname for a catcher.

balk   the failure by a pitcher to continue his pitch to the plate or complete a pickoff attempt, providing his foot is on the rubber. A balk allows runners to advance one base.

ball   1. a baseball. 2. a pitch thrown outside the strike zone.

ballpark   the enclosed field, with fan seating (known as a stadium), where a team plays.

base on balls   a walk, which sends a batter to first base after four balls are thrown outside the strike zone.

batter's box   the white rectangle measuring 4 feet by 6 feet on each side of home plate, where batters must stand while hitting.

batting average   to figure batting average, divide hits by at-bats. This shows how well the batter performs against pitchers.

bench   1. the bench in the dugout or bullpen. 2. nonstarting players who wait in the dugout as substitutes.

brushback   a pitch thrown close to a batter to make him move farther away from home plate.

bullpen   1. the team's group of relief pitchers. 2. the area in foul territory in the outfield or past the outfield fence where pitchers warm up before and during the game.

bunt a slow grounder made by the batter pushing the bat at the ball or letting the pitch hit the bat.

cleanup the fourth-place batter, asked to "clean up" runners on the bases by driving them home.

coach's box a 20-foot-long rectangle in foul territory near first and third base, where coaches are supposed to stand during the game.

complete game one that a pitcher starts and finishes without relief.

curve a pitch that turns in its route to the plate, usually spinning down and away from the hitter.

cycle a single, double, triple, and homer collected in the same game.

designated hitter (DH) a player chosen to take all at-bats for a teammate, usually the pitcher. The player being hit for can remain in the game, unlike one who is replaced by a pinch-hitter. The American League began the rule in 1973.

division three groupings of teams in each of the American and National Leagues. Teams are grouped by their geographical locations.

double a hit in which a batter reaches second base.

double play a series of plays by the defense resulting in two outs. In the most common double play, fielders get the runner on first and the batter out simultaneously.

double steal a play in which two base runners steal bases at the same time.

dugout an enclosed area in foul territory on each side of the field, where teams sit when not playing on the field.

earned run any run scored without the defense making an error.

earned run average the measurement of earned runs allowed by a pitcher in nine innings. To figure an ERA, multiply a pitcher's earned runs by nine, then divide by total innings pitched.

expansion the addition of new teams, expanding the major leagues. From 1901 to 1960, only eight teams each played in the American and National Leagues. In 1998, 16 teams played in the National League and 14 played in the American League.

extra innings additional play if a game is tied after nine innings. If the home team, batting last, breaks the tie, the game is over instantly. If the visitors take the lead, the home team must bat before a winner can be determined.

fielding percentage   how well a fielder responds to game conditions. Add a fielder's assists and putouts, then divide that number by the total number of chances (times the fielder attempted a play).

force play   a play in which a runner must advance a base because of oncoming runners and is put out before reaching the next base. A runner on first base must leave the base for the oncoming batter when the ball is hit. The runner on first can be forced by an infielder catching the ball and touching second base.

forkball   a pitch with a downward curve and little rotation, made by pitchers spreading the index and middle fingers wide across the ball in a "fork."

four-bagger   nickname for a home run, because the hitter gets to touch all four bases or bags.

Gold Glove   award presented to top fielders in each league since 1957.

grand slam   a home run with the bases loaded, creating four runs scored.

hanging curve   the curve ball that doesn't curve well, hanging in mid-air for the batter to hit.

hook slide   also known as a fadeaway, in which the runner slides away from the base, then hooks the base by touching it with his hand, done to avoid the reach of a fielder.

intentional walk   four straight pitches thrown intentionally wide of the plate so the batter has no chance of hitting them.

iron man   a player who plays every day, or with injury. Cal Ripken Jr., who broke Lou Gehrig's record of 2,130 consecutive games played, would be so named.

knuckleball   a slow pitch thrown by gripping the ball with the fingertips or fingernails to avoid rotation.

lead   1. the advantage of having more runs than the other team. 2. the distance a runner moves off a base, preparing to steal or advance on a hit.

left on base runners who are stranded at the end of the inning, without scoring.

lineup 1. starting players. 2. the order in which the starting players will bat.

losing pitcher the pitcher who is credited for being in the game when the winning team scored the go-ahead run.

Most Valuable Player (MVP) the player in each league, at the end of the regular season, who has contributed most to the success of his team. Since 1931, baseball reporters have voted on the winner.

National Baseball Hall of Fame a museum in Cooperstown, New York, honoring retired players with at least 10 years of major league experience. To be elected, players must be named by 75 percent of voters from the Baseball Writers Association of America.

passed ball failure by a catcher to catch a pitch, allowing runners to advance. See also **wild pitch**.

pinch hitter a batter who hits for a teammate. A pinch hitter may remain in the game playing any position. However, the player who is pinch-hit for must leave the game.

pinch runner someone who takes the place of a base runner. The runner who is substituted for cannot return to the game in the next inning.

pitcher's mound the dirt hill where the pitcher stands while throwing to the batter 60 feet, 6 inches away. Beginning in 1903, the mound was no more than 15 inches higher than home plate and the base lines. In 1969, as batting averages dropped, rule changes lowered the high point of the mound to 10 inches.

pitcher's rubber a rubber rectangle, 24 by 6 inches, set in the middle of the pitching mound. Rules require the pitcher to keep a back foot on the rubber until the ball is released.

pop-up slide a slide with a slightly bent back leg, enabling the runner to stand up quickly after reaching a base.

position one of nine defensive spots assigned to players in the field.

postseason a period after the end of the regular season, in which the top-finishing teams play in League Division Series, League Championship Series, and World Series games.

pull hitter a hitter who tends to hit the ball to the side of the field that follows the natural swing of the bat. For example, a right-handed batter usually hits to left field and a left-handed batter to right field. Both are pull hitters.

putout an out credited to a fielder against a batter or runner.

rally a series of hits and runs in one inning.

relay a series of throws from one fielder to another.

retired the state of being put or declared out.

rookie a player in his first year.

rotation 1. how the ball rotates when pitched. 2. the order in which a team uses pitchers to start games, in a group of either four or five.

round-tripper slang for a home run, when a batter gets a trip "round" all the bases.

run batted in (RBI) also known as a "ribbie." RBI credits the effort of the batter in making one or more runs score. A hit, a walk with the bases loaded, a sacrifice bunt, or a sacrifice fly are the most common ways to earn an RBI.

sacrifice bunt a short bunt that brings fielders out of position, allowing runners to advance. Fielders only have time to get the batter out.

sacrifice fly a fly ball that enables a runner to tag up from third base and score.

save a statistic awarded to a relief pitcher who helped his team win. A reliever must have pitched at least three effective innings, entered the game with the possible tying run on base, at bat, or on deck, or have pitched at least one inning with a lead of no more than three runs. Saves have been official stats only since 1969.

scoring position the position of a runner on second or third base, able to score on a hit or a fly ball.

scout a team employee hired to find young talent who could be future major leaguers.

screwball a pitch done by twisting the wrist in the opposite direction of throwing a curve, giving the ball a reverse spin.

shortstop the defensive player stationed between the second baseman and third baseman.

shutout a game in which one team is held scoreless, "shut out" of scoring.

sidearm a pitch delivered with the arm crossing the body below the shoulder.

sinker a pitch that drops as it arrives at home plate.

slider a fastball that curves just a little before it reaches home plate.

split-fingered fastball a pitch delivered with the ball held between the widely spread index and middle fingers, that drops sharply at home plate.

spring training a period of preparation beginning in February in warm-weather places such as Florida and Arizona. Teams hold practices before the regular season, choosing which players will begin the season with the team.

suicide squeeze the attempt by a runner from third base to reach home plate as the pitch is thrown. The batter's job is to bunt any pitch away from the catcher, who wants to tag the runner out. If the batter can't squeeze the runner home, the runner risks a likely out.

strike out the retirement of a batter after receiving three strikes.

switch-hitter a player who can hit right-handed or left-handed.

tag to put a runner out by touching him with the glove, or a bare hand holding the ball.

take to not swing at a pitch.

triple a hit in which the batter advances all the way to third base, without the defense making any errors.

umpire an official who decides major rules, such as balls and strikes, fair and foul balls, and which runners are safe or out. For regular-season games, four umpires work beside home plate and the three bases.

walk   the right of a batter to advance to first base after receiving four pitches that were not ruled strikes.

wild pitch   a pitch too wild for a catcher to catch, allowing runners to advance.

windup   a pitcher's motion before delivering a pitch.

World Series   a contest in which the champions of the American and National Leagues play each other. The winner of four out of seven games is named the World Champion. Held since 1903 (except in 1904 because of an uncooperative team manager, and 1994, during a conflict between players and owners over money).

FOR MORE INFORMATION

Books

Conlin, Bill. *The Rutledge Book of Baseball*. New York: Rutledge Press, 1981.

Gutman, Dan. *Baseball's Greatest Games*. New York: Puffin Books, 1996.

Sullivan, George. *Glovemen: Twenty-Seven of Baseball's Greatest*. New York: Atheneum, 1996.

Books for Older Readers

Dickson, Paul. *The Joy of Keeping Score: How Scoring the Game Has Influenced and Enhanced the History of Baseball*. San Diego: Harcourt Brace, 1996.

Gutman, Dan. *Banana Bats and Ding-Dong Balls: A Century of Unique Baseball Inventions*. New York: Macmillan, 1995.

McCarver, Tim with Danny Peary. *Tim McCarver's Baseball for Brain Surgeons and Other Fans: Understanding and Interpreting the Game So You Can Watch It Like a Pro*. New York: Villard Books, 1998.

Internet Resources

www.majorleaguebaseball.com
The official site of Major League Baseball, all links to team web sites are included.

www.bigleaguers.com

The Major League Baseball Players' Association sponsors this site, which gives lots of biographical information.

www.fastball.com

This is a fun, informative site for all types of fans, covering baseball from all angles.

INDEX

Page numbers in *italics* refer to illustrations.